Fantasy Landscapes
in
Watercolour

STUART LITTLEJOHN

SEARCH PRESS

First published in Great Britain 2009

Search Press Limited
Wellwood, North Farm Road,
Tunbridge Wells, Kent TN2 3DR

Text copyright © Stuart Littlejohn 2009

Photographs by Debbie Patterson, Search Press Studio.

Photographs and design copyright © Search Press Ltd. 2009

ISBN: 978-1-84448-377-8

The Publishers and author can accept no responsibility for
any consequences arising from the information, advice or
instructions given in this publication.

The Publishers would like to thank Winsor & Newton for
supplying some of the materials used in this book.

Suppliers
If you have difficulty in obtaining any of the materials or
equipment mentioned in this book, then please visit the Search
Press website for details of suppliers: www.searchpress.com

Publishers' note
All the step-by-step photographs in this book feature the
author, Stuart Littlejohn, demonstrating his watercolour
painting techniques. No models have been used.

There are references to animal hair brushes in this book. It
is the Publishers' custom to recommend synthetic materials
as substitutes for animal products wherever possible. There
is now a large range of brushes available made from artificial
fibres, and they are satisfactory substitutes for those made
from natural fibres.

Printed in Malaysia.

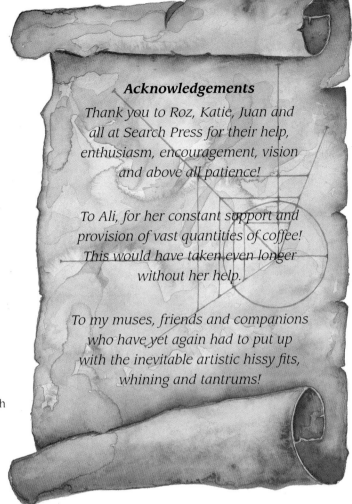

Acknowledgements
*Thank you to Roz, Katie, Juan and
all at Search Press for their help,
enthusiasm, encouragement, vision
and above all patience!*

*To Ali, for her constant support and
provision of vast quantities of coffee!
This would have taken even longer
without her help.*

*To my muses, friends and companions
who have yet again had to put up
with the inevitable artistic hissy fits,
whining and tantrums!*

Dedication
This book is especially dedicated to Jasmine. xxx

Cover:
The Sword and the Stone
*Fantasy landscapes like this allow you the freedom to combine
elements from the real world with those from myths, legends
and your own imagination. Here, a sword is left as an offering
outside an ancient tumulus, from whose depths a mysterious
light shines out.*

Page 1:
The Towers
*This picture represents the way in which the distinction
between natural and man-made structures can become blurred
in fantasy art.*

Opposite:
Sunset
*The ancient tree and stone guard the entrance to another world.
The appeal of fantasy landscape painting depends as much on
what is imagined as on what is actually present.*

Contents

Introduction

We all create fantasy worlds, either in our waking imagination or within dreams. From lost cities to vast plains and jungles, ice-capped mountains to the very underworld itself! This book will help make some of these imagined vistas more real, giving you a jumping-off point, some guidelines to techniques and short cuts that will set you on the path to creating your own, unique worlds. As always, the most important part of this process is to have fun. Let your imagination run riot, do not worry about making mistakes, and everything and anything is possible.

Feel free to build on the guidelines given in this book. If a technique I describe does not work for you, adapt it and experiment. Inspiration is all around you and can be gathered from books, magazines, television, cinema or the internet, as well as your surroundings. Try and get into the habit of always carrying a sketchbook or digital camera wherever you go. Collect interesting objects that stir your imagination: stones, shells, bones, feathers, twisted bits of wood – whatever catches your eye. Sometimes tiny details can be the catalyst for an entire landscape, if scaled up. Very soon you will have your own library of reference material. Look closely too at the work of other artists; study their techniques and what has influenced them. This can open your mind to different ways of seeing things.

Hopefully this book will open a door for you. Explore strange new worlds, and above all have fun!

Bridge Over the Gorge
The power of this painting lies in the unusual perspective from which the scene is viewed, accentuating the depth of the gorge and the enormity of the rocks. Scale and perspective can bc used to great effect in fantasy landscape paintings (see page 14). I got the idea for this painting from remembered images of thc launching of Saturn 5 rockets for the Apollo Moon Missions, with all the gantries, walkways and tubes linking the rocket to the launch tower.

Materials

Art materials can be very expensive and there is a vast choice of paints, brushes and paper on the market, as well as the extra items you might need such as craft knives, erasers, drawing boards – the list goes on. It is best not to dive in and buy everything you think you might need straightaway. To begin with just concentrate on the basics: half a dozen good quality watercolour brushes of various sizes, a pad of medium-weight watercolour paper, a dozen or so tubes of watercolour paint and a selection of pencils of differing hardness should be enough to get you started.

PAINTS

There is a vast range of watercolours available, from the very cheap to the extremely expensive blocks of the finest pigments. I find tubes the most convenient to use, and there is a wide choice of colours. Initially, aim for about a dozen colours that cover the spectrum. Include in this the primaries (red, yellow and blue) as well as some white gouache – this is more opaque than watercolour and is ideal for adding highlights in your paintings as well as hiding mistakes.

PALETTE

This can be an elaborate ceramic mixing dish, with separate wells for individual colours and a larger area for mixing, or else a much cheaper, plastic version. If all else fails, a plain white plate or saucer works just as well.

BRUSHES

When buying paintbrushes you will probably be faced with a bewildering choice of sizes and types. You have to choose between sable, synthetic or a mix of both, as well as differing sizes, from what appears to be a single hair to the equivalent of a wallpaper brush. You do get what you pay for. The higher quality brushes will last longer if looked after and will give a better result, but you do not want to bankrupt yourself straightaway! My personal preference is for pure sable brushes, but they are expensive and for this reason synthetic brushes are probably the best to begin with. You will eventually find which kind of brush suits your way of working. I use a mix of sizes, from a tiny size 0000 to the larger size 4 for detailed work, and up to sizes 7 or 8 for larger areas and backgrounds.

A selection of the brushes I use for watercolour painting.

PAINTING SURFACES

Paper is just one type of surface you can paint on. Try experimenting with different surfaces. Wood and medium-density fibreboard (MDF) can give a wonderfully hard, smooth finish. Other types of wood might well have a particular grain which could enhance your finished picture. When you have found a piece of a suitable size, sand it down and prime it with two or more coats of white matt emulsion paint. When each coat is dry, use fine-grade sandpaper to get rid of any imperfections. Do this again when you have applied the final coat. The white primer will give an added lustre to your completed painting. Using off-cuts of wood or board in this way is also a cost-effective method of trying out new techniques before moving on to the more precious watercolour paper.

Which type of paper you choose has important effects on the finished piece. Watercolour papers range from very smooth (often described as HP, or hot pressed) to rough and heavily textured (described as NOT or cold pressed). Throughout this book I have used 300gsm (140lb) and 190gsm (90lb) cold pressed NOT papers.

You will also need a sketchbook for sketching out your ideas and noting down anything that inspires you, and tracing paper, which comes either in a pad or in sheets, and is used to transfer your finished design to your watercolour paper.

STRETCHING PAPER

I always stretch my watercolour paper before I start, as it keeps the paper taut and stops it cockling when water is applied. To stretch paper you will need a wooden board (I use an A2 piece of thick marine ply), your paper and some brown paper sealing tape. Soak your paper liberally on both sides with water and, using a sponge or cloth, dribble water on to your board underneath where you want your paper to sit. Lay the paper on to the board and gently expel any air bubbles from beneath the sheet. Do not press or scrub the paper too hard as the surface might get damaged. When the paper is flat, tear off a strip of sealing tape a little longer than the longest side of your paper sheet, wet the tape with the sponge and stick it firmly along the edge of the paper and down on to the board. Try and make sure the tape is well stuck and repeat on the other three sides of the sheet.

When you have finished, let the paper dry naturally. Do not be tempted to hurry it along with a hairdryer, as it might pull off the board and you will have to start again! At this point you might be alarmed to see your beautiful sheet of paper begin to acquire ridges and bubbles, but do not worry – as it dries it shrinks, and should be pulled taut ready to paint on. Do not remove the paper yet – paint on it while it is still secured to the board, and remove it once the finished painting has dried.

OTHER MATERIALS

Pencils and sharpeners: a good selection of pencils is essential. You will need a hard (H), a medium (HB or F) and a soft (B). For very fine drawing, a 2H or even a 3H is advisable, particularly for painting over your underlying drawing; the harder the line, the less likely it is to smudge when you apply the paint and your colours will stay cleaner. Keep your pencils well sharpened with a scalpel, craft knife or pencil sharpener.

Eraser: a soft putty eraser is ideal as it can be shaped to a fine point if needed. Adhesive putty (the type you use for attaching posters to walls) also works very well.

Kitchen paper: use this for lifting out paint or excess water from your work.

Pair of compasses: for drawing circles accurately.

Hairdryer: this speeds up the drying process; you can achieve some interesting effects by using a blast of hot air to move the paint around on the paper.

Water pot: you can buy water pots especially made for artists, but alternatively a jam jar is ideal. I use a small glass jar that originally held whole-grain mustard!

Brown paper sealing tape: this has water-soluble gum on one side and is used for attaching your watercolour paper to a wooden board before stretching (see page 8).

Ruler and set square: these are useful, when making your initial drawing, for ensuring lines are straight and for achieving true verticals and horizontals, for example the sides of towers and other artificial structures, and horizon lines.

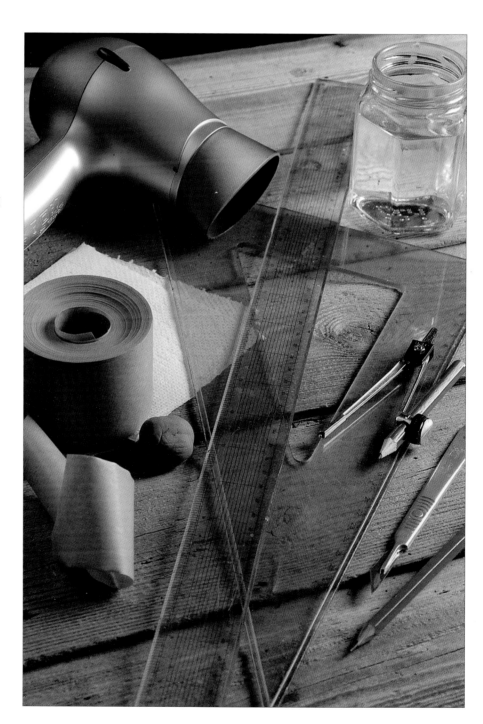

Colour

There is an amazing range of watercolour pigments available, and you can mix practically any colour you want from the three primary colours of red, yellow and blue. Add white to lighten a colour or blue/black to darken it. Rather than mixing colours on your palette, allow the paints to mix on the paper as you paint. You can create some stunning effects as the colours blend into each other. Work with the way the paint flows naturally rather than against it, 'pushing' it around using a blast of air from a hairdryer to control the effect if necessary. Do not be afraid to experiment with mixing. See which combinations of colour work well together and create test pieces for future reference; in other words, play with the paint!

The use of colour in landscape painting is very important to get a sense of depth and distance. Generally darker colours will appear closer whilst lighter, paler shades will recede. There are exceptions to this: any colour that is highly saturated (or very bright) will tend to advance towards the viewer, whereas warm foreground colours will draw the viewer forwards, as will cool but intense colours. Colour also plays an important role in defining the mood of your painting. This is explored in more detail on pages 16–17.

TIP
Always make sure you mix enough colour for the area you are painting – there is nothing worse than creating the most wonderful shade for a sky and then running out halfway through applying your wash and being unable to quite match it when you mix another batch!

A colour wheel shows the relationship of the three primary colours: red, yellow and blue. The primaries cannot be created by mixing any other pigments together. Mixing the primaries creates the secondaries: green, purple and orange. The colour opposite each of these is their complementary colour. Complementary pairs generally work well when placed next to each other in a painting, enhancing each other's appearance and giving a sense of drama to the picture as a whole.

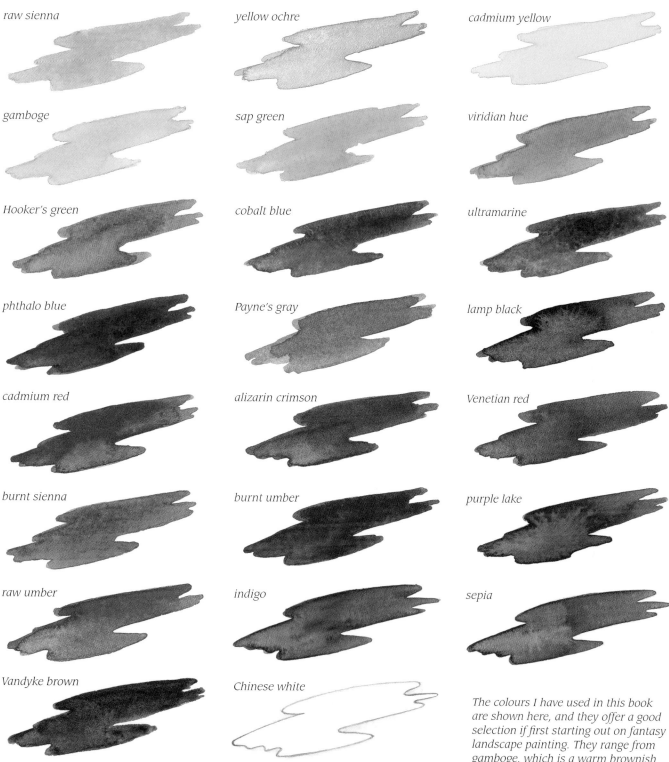

raw sienna

yellow ochre

cadmium yellow

gamboge

sap green

viridian hue

Hooker's green

cobalt blue

ultramarine

phthalo blue

Payne's gray

lamp black

cadmium red

alizarin crimson

Venetian red

burnt sienna

burnt umber

purple lake

raw umber

indigo

sepia

Vandyke brown

Chinese white

The colours I have used in this book are shown here, and they offer a good selection if first starting out on fantasy landscape painting. They range from gamboge, which is a warm brownish yellow, through to Vandyke brown, a strong nutty brown. The variations in between give a vast range of options. I also use white gouache, which is thicker and more opaque than watercolour, to add bright highlights and sparkles. It is also very useful for covering over mistakes, as the colour underneath will not bleed through!

One of the most exciting aspects of fantasy painting is the fact that you can use any colour you wish for skies, foliage, rocks and creatures. For example, in this book my skies have ranged from a burning cadmium yellow and red to a mysterious cobalt blue, ultramarine and phthalo blue mix. Foliage and trees can take on unnatural hues, water can reflect exotic skies, and figures can blend into their natural surroundings by acquiring the tones and colours of the landscape. Experiment with colour, and allow your imagination free rein.

11

Inspiration

It is very hard to sit down before a blank sheet of paper and create a scene spontaneously. We all need some inspiration to get us started. As I mentioned briefly in the introduction, there are many sources which can kick start the process, including the cinema, TV adverts, magazines and the internet. Looking at everyday objects in a slightly different way can be very useful too; I was always struck by how the insides of a computer look like some vast futuristic city if you get down close enough – the components become buildings with an almost brutalist style of architecture and the circuit boards become the street plan. It is a case of keeping your mind open to whatever comes your way!

All sorts of images have been used for inspiration for the paintings in this book. Mountains, dramatic skies, rocks, bones, trees – all can help fire the imagination. Try to get into the habit of taking a camera or sketchbook with you wherever you go – you will be amazed at how many everyday scenes and objects would be equally at home in a fantasy landscape!

For the Gorge Temple pictured opposite, I combined a photograph of a sunset taken on the North Devon Coast with a model I built that was based on the Temple of Vespasian in Pompeii, adding the gryphon-like guardians along the way. Mixing elements from different sources can give fantastic results, and can often lead on to other things.

The two photographs on the left were combined using Photoshop to create the image in the centre. I then varied this image by replacing the background with a steep gorge and altering the colours to rich reds, browns and oranges. Sketches, like those shown above, were also used to develop my ideas further.

Gorge Temple

Composition

When composing a picture try and create a 'pathway' for the eye to follow; by arranging your chosen elements carefully, you can create interest and the odd surprise, finally focusing on the most important part of the picture. How the elements are set out also lends emotional impact and helps with the 'story' that you are trying to illustrate.

PERSPECTIVE

Painting is, essentially, the representation of three dimensions on a two-dimensional surface. To do this successfully, you need to know a little about perspective. In its broadest sense, perspective refers to the fact that objects appear to get smaller as they recede into a background, and that an object's dimensions along the line of sight appear to be shorter than those across the line of sight, resulting in foreshortening. Perspective also refers to the angle at which the elements in the picture are positioned relative to the person viewing them, which can be from above or below, directly in front or from one side or the other.

Understanding and using perspective is important when composing paintings, even though the theory behind it can be a little daunting. It gives your pictures a solid grounding in space and of course you can then start to play around with it, to bend the rules, and to exaggerate height, depth and distance. This can be used to dramatic effect in fantasy landscape painting.

The rock on the right has been drawn face-on and is viewed from below, accentuating its height and dramatic impact. This perspective is also known as three-point perspective, as the receding parallel lines comprising the piece converge at three points – A, B and C. These are also known as vanishing points.

Nonlinear scenes, which contain no parallel lines, are common in landscapes, for example mountain ranges, valleys and plains. Such scenes, like the one shown along the top of the page, are said to be painted in zero-point perspective because there are no

vanishing points. In one-point perspective, every line converges at a single point, usually on the horizon, and in two-point perspective there are two sets of parallel lines and therefore two vanishing points.

An example of how a composition is developed in two-point perspective is shown below. I started with a very rough thumbnail sketch of my idea, trying to gauge the overall feeling of the picture. I then moved on to a more detailed treatment. I wanted to emphasise the zigzag path leading up to the gateway, so I used two-point perspective to construct the path and also to give form to the tower itself. The final picture is of the finished vignette. I have deliberately let the edges of the colour bleed out to give a softer, less enclosed feel to the painting (see also page 42).

The Wizard's Tower

The moonlit zigzag path draws the viewer into the tiny gateway at the base of the tower, which is backlit by the huge pale moon. The use of light and shade adds to the atmosphere of the pivce (see pages 16–17).

Mood & atmosphere

It is almost as important what you leave out of a painting as what you include. Allowing the imagination of the viewer to contribute to the picture is a very effective way of enhancing the impact of your work. Details can be obscured by mist, snow, overwhelming darkness or blinding light. Half-seen objects can take on a different form entirely within the imagination, and the same feature can look very different depending on whether it is day or night, in sun or in rain.

These pages show how the same picture can dramatically change its mood and atmosphere by simply by changing the palette that you use.

This first picture shows a burial mound and standing stone at high summer. The strong yellow sky suggests sunset and the predominant colour of the land is bright green. The band of pale pinks and blues used for the mountain range in the background gives the piece depth.

The stone and burial mound under a clear starry sky, with a bright moon just visible behind the branches of the tree. The moonlight illuminates the broad landscape but throws the tree, mound and stone into shadow. Dark blues and greens predominate, giving the scene a gloomy, sombre air.

The mound and stone in the depths of winter. I have used a limited palette of blues, greys and browns and the shapes of the stones and the mound are softened by the snow. The sense of silence that comes with a heavy snowfall, when all sound becomes muffled, is strong.

This bleak interpretation of the scene shows it enshrouded in mist, creating a mysterious, ghostly atmosphere. To achieve this effect I used watery mixes of blues, greens and yellows. Moorlands have a similar feel, especially early in the morning, when you could be forgiven for thinking they are gateways to other realms!

Mountain Cave

In this picture I wanted to give a sense of great distance and scale as well as a more intimate and human-sized foreground. The eye is led from the runestone to the small cave where something is mysteriously concealed, then on up the path to the great fortress crag that over time has weathered into its environment. Beyond is another similar mountain (is it natural or is it another castle?). The icy blues and purples of the far distant mountain range and the three tiny figures on the path suggest the immensity of the landscape.

TIP

Remember to stretch your watercolour paper before starting the project (see page 8).

1 Draw the image directly on to the watercolour paper using a sharp F pencil, or transfer it following the instructions given below. Use a pair of compasses to draw in the moon.

TIP

If you are not confident at drawing, trace the image on to tracing paper, and go over the lines on the back of the tracing using a fairly soft pencil. Position the tracing face up on your watercolour paper and rub over the lines of the image firmly using either a pencil or the end of a spoon. The image will be transferred to the paper.

YOU WILL NEED

300gsm (140lb) cold pressed NOT paper, size A3 (30 x 42cm; 11¾ x 16½in)

F grade drawing pencil

Putty eraser

Pair of compasses

Paintbrushes: 13mm (½in) and 6mm (¼in) flat brushes; sizes 1, 4 and 6 round brushes

Kitchen paper

Hairdryer

Water pot

Watercolour paints: cobalt blue, phthalo blue, ultramarine, cadmium red, Payne's gray, indigo, sap green, yellow ochre, Hooker's green, Vandyke brown, burnt umber, sepia, burnt sienna, lamp black

Gouache: permanent white

2 Dampen the sky using the larger flat brush, avoiding the moon. Do not be too concerned if some of the water bleeds into the mountains. Pick up a watery mix of cobalt blue and apply the base colour to the sky, leaving a narrow gap around the tops of the mountains. Continue to drop in water to create patches of paler colour.

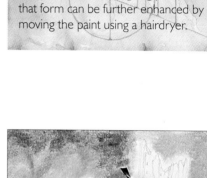

3 Drop in patches of dilute phthalo blue, allowing them to blend naturally with the cobalt blue.

TIP

Do not apply a flat wash of colour to skies as this will create a dull, two-dimensional painting. Instead, dab wet paint on to a wet surface (known as the wet-into-wet technique), allowing it to flow across the paper and settle naturally to create patches of colour. Move the paint around as you work to prevent 'puddles' and dry patches. The beautiful and intriguing patterns that form can be further enhanced by moving the paint using a hairdryer.

4 Darken the top of the sky further using ultramarine, again applied in patches mixed with plenty of water.

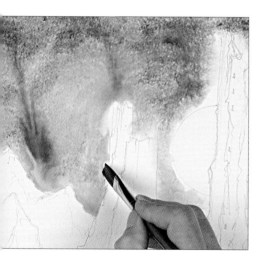

5 Add a pink glow to the horizon by applying cadmium red to the lower part of the sky, around the mountains. Allow the colour to blend gently with the blue.

6 Change to a size 6 round brush. Pick up a small amount of permanent white gouache and paint carefully around the edge of the moon and around the edges of the mountains here and there to give them a luminous quality. Allow the paint to bleed into the blue.

TIP

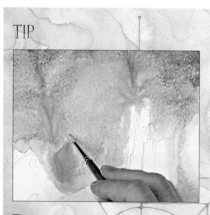

The way the paint had settled meant that by pushing the gouache into it I could create swirling patterns in the sky. Working with the random patterns formed naturally by the paint in this way can create stunning effects, particularly in fantasy art.

7 Dry the paint with a hairdryer. Use the hot air to move the paint around, hence further enhancing the patterns formed in the sky by the drying paint. Soften any hard edges that appear with a clean, damp brush.

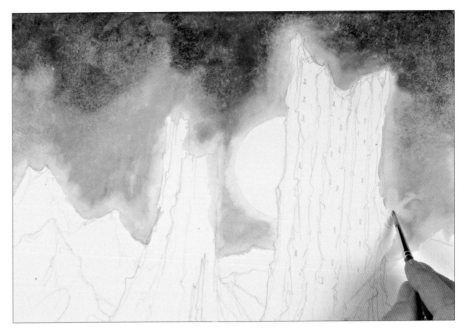

8 Strengthen the top part of the sky using ultramarine. Dab it on gently, pulling it down to blend into the lower part. Add more water to the mix as you approach the horizon to lighten it. Add a little more phthalo blue and white gouache to the bottom of the sky. Allow the paint to dry naturally.

9 Continuing with the size 6 round brush, paint the runestone using a watery mix of Payne's gray. While it is still wet, add a little indigo and allow it to blend with the grey.

10 Add patches of sap green at the base of the runestone and pull the colour up towards the top, blending it with the grey to resemble moss.

11 Place patches of yellow ochre here and there to mimic lichen, particularly on the top of the runestone and down the left-hand side.

12 Strengthen the grass at the base of the runestone using sap green, and darken it here and there with Hooker's green. Paint in the shapes of the blades of grass.

13 Place yellow ochre around the base and blend it into the green, aiming for an interesting mix of colours and tones. Allow the paint to dry.

14 Lay a wash of Vandyke brown over the stones leading to the entrance of the cave, then blend in some yellow ochre.

15 Use Payne's gray to define the lower edges of the stones, then darken the base of the stones using burnt umber. Extend the burnt umber into the foreground, lightening it as you pull it forward.

16 Paint in the area in the foreground under the runestone using yellow ochre, followed by Vandyke brown and Payne's gray. Blend the colours on the paper to create a mottled effect.

17 Now that the base colours are in place, start to strengthen the painting and add detail. Put a strong shadow down the side of the runestone using a mix of Payne's gray and Vandyke brown. Strengthen the grass using Payne's gray mixed with a little Hooker's green.

18 Using the smaller flat brush, lay in the area of ground just behind the runestone with a light wash of Payne's gray.

19 Brush in some yellow ochre and sap green, laying the colour in horizontal stripes following the pattern of the ground. Allow the colours to blend on the paper, and soften the edges if necessary.

20 Add colour and definition to the cliff face using a wash of Payne's gray followed by Vandyke brown and yellow ochre. Use vertical brush strokes to help define the contours.

TIP

When applying a base colour over a large area, lay the brush strokes in the same direction as the main features, for example the vertical rocks that make up a cliff face or the horizontal stripes formed by the fields in a landscape. Defining the shape and contours of the land in this way will form a solid base on which to build a strong, three-dimensional painting.

21 Complete this section of the painting by strengthening the foreground in front of the runestone using Vandyke brown and Payne's gray.

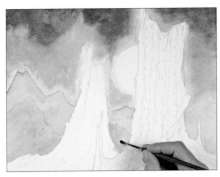

22 Turning now to the background, make a very pale purple mix of cadmium red and cobalt blue and paint in the mountains furthest away in the distance. Make a bluer mix and paint in the mountains further forward. Dab the paint on patchily, working carefully round the two foreground crags.

23 Change to the size 6 round brush and put in the shadows on the right-hand sides of the far distant crags using cobalt blue. Soften the edges of the shadows using a clean, damp brush. Put in some tiny patches of white gouache where the light from the left is hitting the tops of the mountains.

24 Put some white into the tops of the closer mountains, dragging the paint down in sweeping curves to their base. Place the highlights to suggest a light source on the left of the picture.

25 Strengthen the darkest parts of the mountains using a mix of cobalt blue and cadmium red, and put in the strong right-hand shadows on the mountains that are furthest forwards.

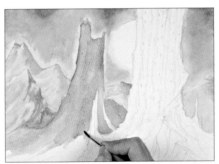

26 Apply the base colour to the smaller of the two main crags. Start with a fairly dark, watery mix of Payne's gray, dragging the paint down from the top of the peak and fading it out slightly at the base. Add some streaks of yellow ochre and cobalt blue, allowing them to mix freely with the grey.

27 Change to the larger flat brush and apply a base of Payne's gray to the main crag. Use a slightly darker mix than in the previous step. Add in some vertical streaks of yellow ochre, and allow them to bleed into the grey.

28 Add some cobalt blue in-between the yellow, then extend the base of the crag into the foreground using a watery mix of Payne's gray. Deepen the colour of the rocks to the right of the path, which are in shadow. Leave the path free of paint. Add more yellow and blue to the foreground on the left of the path to help define the contours of the rocks.

29 Turning now to the mid-ground, lay on a light wash of yellow ochre, then drag across some stripes of Payne's gray followed by a little cobalt blue, following the contours of the land. Allow the colours to blend into each other at the edges.

30 Paint over the cave using yellow ochre, then define the stones by blending some Payne's gray into the lower parts of the stones and Vandyke brown into the upper parts.

31 Paint in the grass in the lower right-hand corner of the picture using sap green, followed by Hooker's green to deepen the colour. Add a little yellow ochre at the base and some Payne's gray at the top.

32 Change to the size 6 round brush and place a fairly dark mix of Payne's gray over the entrance to the cave, allowing it to bleed into the adjacent stones. Use the same mix to deepen the shadows between the stones. Allow the paint to dry.

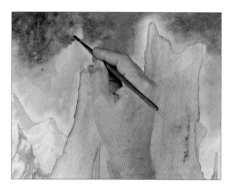

33 Strengthen the sky by first softening any hard edges that have formed using a damp size 4 round brush, then changing to a size 6 brush and applying a strong mix of ultramarine to the top part of the sky. Drag the colour downwards, stopping just short of the edges of the mountains. Use a damp brush to blend the colour with the lighter blues underneath and to soften any hard edges.

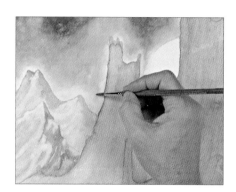

34 Add more white around the edges of the mountains and the moon, and blend it in using a clean, damp brush.

35 Paint the moon with a fairly watery mix of cobalt blue. Dab on some patches of Payne's gray and a little white gouache, allowing them to blend naturally with the blue. Carefully smooth the edge of the moon as you work to retain a crisp outline.

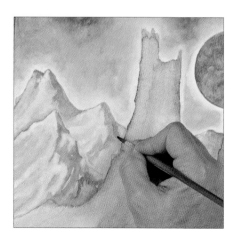

36 Strengthen and define the edges of the distant mountains using cobalt blue applied with the tip of the brush, and accentuate the shadows. Soften in the colour with a damp brush.

TIP

To achieve a sense of depth in your painting, you need to build up and strengthen the colours. This can be done as many times as necessary to achieve the desired result. Always soften in the colours as you work using a clean, damp brush to avoid hard edges.

37 Start to build up the detailing on the smaller of the two main crags. Using cobalt blue, lay in strong, uneven shadows running from top to bottom. Soften them in with a damp brush.

38 Add deeper shadows using Payne's gray, particularly at the top of the crag and down the right-hand side. Take the grey down beyond the base of the mountain to help differentiate it from the mountains in the background.

39 Add white highlights, mainly down the left-hand side, using white gouache, and deepen the darkest shadows on the right and at the base with Payne's gray.

40 Turning now to the main crag, put in the strong, vertical shadows using indigo. Paint carefully around the tiny windows. Retain the shadows' hard edges to bring the mountain forward and accentuate its rough, jagged appearance.

41 Pull the shadows down into the rocks at the foot of the crag.

42 Paint in the lighter areas of the crag using yellow ochre followed by white gouache. Change to a size 1 round brush and use the white paint to put light in the windows.

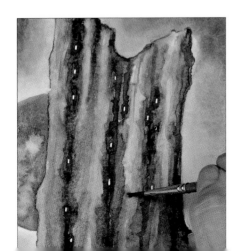

TIP

Lift out excess colour by dabbing it with a screwed up piece of kitchen paper.

43 Continue with the size 1 brush and use indigo to strengthen the shadows in the deepest parts of the crag, painting carefully around the windows. Soften in the shadows using a damp, size 4 brush.

44 Darken the area at the base of the main crag, to the right of the path, using a wash of Vandyke brown followed by patches of indigo. Place the darkest shadows at the back and soften the paint in with a damp brush.

45 Strengthen the area to the left of the path using yellow ochre applied with the size 4 brush. Work the colour between the shadows, overlapping them slightly.

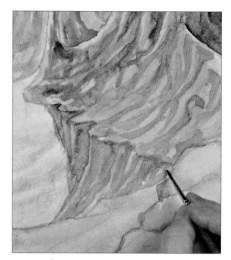

46 Deepen the shadows at the foot of the crag using indigo, accentuating the shapes of the rocks, and soften them in with clean water. Use the same colour to add deeper shadows to the cliff face and under the overhang.

47 Define the main spike (in the middle of the picture) by painting the background around it using white gouache, then advance the spike further using Vandyke brown to build up the shadows.

48 While the paint is drying, put in the suggestion of a forest in the valley using a size 4 round brush and Hooker's green mixed with a little indigo. Use short, upright brush strokes to mimic the shape of the trees, and alter the mix slightly as you work to obtain variation in colour and tone.

49 Strengthen the stones around the entrance to the cave with patches of Vandyke brown and sap green. Fill the cave with indigo followed by cobalt blue, extending the colour into the cracks between the stones. Apply the paint with a size 6 round brush. Finally, add shadows to the undersides of the stones using Payne's gray. Allow the paint to dry.

TIP
Dry brushing is a way of adding texture. It is most effective on textured watercolour paper. Pick up the paint with a dry flat brush, remove any excess by wiping it on a piece of kitchen paper, then rub the colour on to a dry surface.

50 Use dry brushing (see above) to add texture to the stones. First rub on some Payne's gray using the smaller flat brush, then rub a layer of sepia over the top.

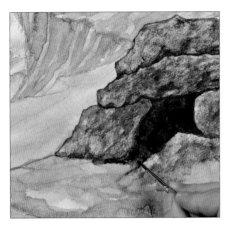

51 Bring the cave further forward by outlining the stones using sepia mixed with Payne's gray applied with a size 1 brush. Change to the size 4 brush and deepen the cave entrance using Payne's gray.

52 Add texture to the stones in front of the cave. Dry brush on some burnt sienna followed by burnt umber using the smaller flat brush. Blend the colours into the base of the cave. Outline the stones with a mix of Vandyke brown and burnt sienna using the tip of the size 1 brush.

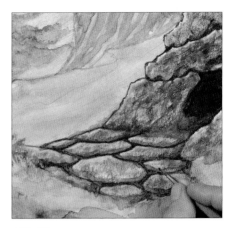

53 Using the size 4 round brush, darken the cave further with lamp black, leaving a light patch in the lower part. With the same brush put more shadows into the stones using Payne's gray, then add highlights using white gouache. Soften the edges and remove any excess paint with kitchen paper if necessary.

54 Build up the colour of the ground just behind the cave using sap green, Hooker's green and yellow ochre. Use smooth brush strokes to contrast with the highly textured features in the foreground. Vary the mix slightly as you work and lay on the colours in bands, following the contours of the land. Dry each band of colour with a hairdryer before moving on to the next to emphasise the striped effect.

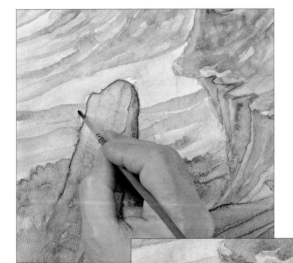

55 Strengthen the colours of the land lying behind the forest using a watery mix of yellow ochre and Payne's gray. Work in horizontal stripes, as before, building up the colour in layers and drying each section with a hairdryer before moving on to the next.

56 Returning to the cliff face, use yellow ochre mixed with Payne's gray to introduce more colour and deepen the shadows, particularly towards the top. Add a hint of white towards the base of the cliff to make it recede a little.

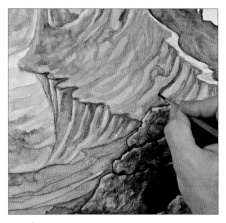

57 Lay a wash of burnt sienna over the area to the left of the path, then work the same colour into the area on the right to 'lift' the shadows. Mix Payne's gray with a little burnt sienna and use it to define the edge of the path and the lines of the contours on the left.

58 Use a dark mix of Payne's gray to define the entrance at the end of the path. Place highlights on the path and strengthen those on the area to the left using white gouache.

59 With a size 1 round brush, draw the detailing on the runestone using a mix of burnt umber and Payne's gray.

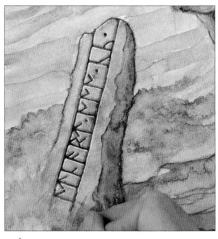

60 Place a shadow to the left of each line using a paler version of the same mix, and a white highlight to the right to give depth to the carvings. Soften any hard edges using a clean, damp brush.

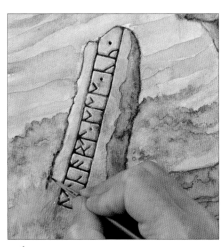

61 Darken the carved lines further with Payne's gray, and use a mix of Hooker's green and Payne's gray to strengthen the left-hand edge of the runestone to pull it further forwards, away from the background.

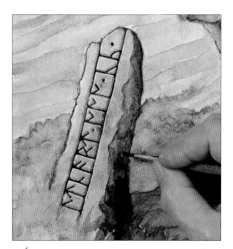

62 Further enhance the three-dimensional effect by deepening the shadow on the right-hand side of the runestone with Payne's gray mixed with burnt umber. Apply the paint with a size 4 brush.

63 Using the dry brush technique (see page 25), apply burnt umber to the front of the runestone to create texture.

64 Give further definition to the grass below the runestone using a mix of Hooker's green, sap green and yellow ochre. Use short, upwards brush strokes to mimic the blades of grass and soften the colour in at the base. Dab in some patches of yellow ochre to add colour and tone.

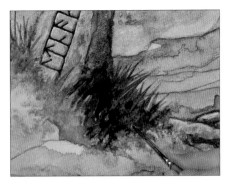

65 Deepen the colour of the clump of grass on the right of the runestone using a mix of Payne's gray and Hooker's green. Strengthen the area around it using Hooker's green, yellow ochre and sap green.

66 Strengthen the grass in the bottom right of the picture using the same colours and brush in the blades of grass growing around the base of the cave.

67 Lay a light green wash over the stones at the cave's entrance to tie them in with the rest of the foreground. Dry brush over the large foreground rock using burnt umber applied with the smaller flat brush.

68 Place a magical sparkle in the cave entrance. Use the size 1 brush and white gouache. Begin with a central dot, surround it with a small ring of white, then pull out the rays from the centre using a clean, damp brush.

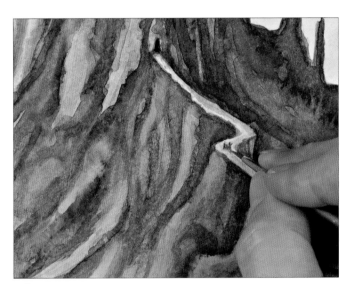

69 To add a sense of scale, place three tiny figures on the path.

70 Finally, dot in the stars using white gouache applied with the tip of the size 1 brush.

Wizard's Cavern

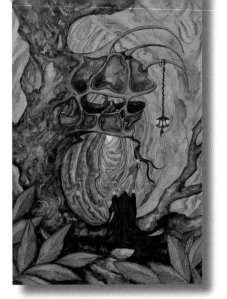

In contrast to the previous painting, this reverses the sense of scale by focusing the eye into the depths of a green, living cavern in which the figures are dwarfed by the trees and leaves of their environment. Manipulating scale is a useful tool when creating fantasy art. The dominant shades of green form a backdrop for the vivid scarlets, blues and golds of the wizard's cloak and the balcony which seems to be a natural extension to the tree.

TIP

Remember to stretch your watercolour paper before starting the project (see page 8).

1 Draw the image directly on to the watercolour paper using a sharp F pencil, or transfer it following the instructions on page 18.

TIP

In pictures like this, in which there is one very dominant background colour, it can save time if the details, in this case the figures and the balcony, are masked out with masking fluid. The dominant colour is then applied over the whole of the painting. When the background has dried, the masking fluid is gently rubbed off, leaving the details clear for the brighter more vibrant colours to be applied.

YOU WILL NEED

300gsm (140lb) cold pressed NOT paper, size A3 (30 x 42cm; 11¾ x 16½in)

F grade drawing pencil

Putty eraser

Paintbrushes: ⅝in (16mm) flat brush; sizes 0000, 1, 3, 4 and 6 round brushes

Kitchen paper

Hairdryer

Water pot

Watercolour paints: cobalt blue, phthalo blue, cadmium red, cadmium yellow, alizarin crimson, Payne's gray, indigo, sap green, yellow ochre, viridian hue, Hooker's green, Vandyke brown, sepia, burnt sienna, lamp black, burnt umber

Gouache: permanent white

TIP

You need to start building up the colours in this painting from an early stage to achieve a real sense of depth. The predominance of green could result in a flat, two-dimensional picture without marked variations in tone.

2 Lay a light green wash over the drawing, without dampening the paper first. Use the flat brush, and apply sap green and viridian hue in patches, allowing them to mix on the paper. Leave the figures white.

3 Deepen the inner part of the cavern to bring the foreground forward. Paint in the direction of the lines on the drawing to define the contours of the cave. Dry the painting with a hairdryer.

4 Using a size 6 round brush, put in the leaves in the foreground. Make a fairly watery mix of sap green and dab the paint on so that it dries patchily (this creates a more interesting effect than a plain wash of colour).

5 Mix together some viridian hue and sap green and use it to darken the main tree trunk and the outer part of the cavern.

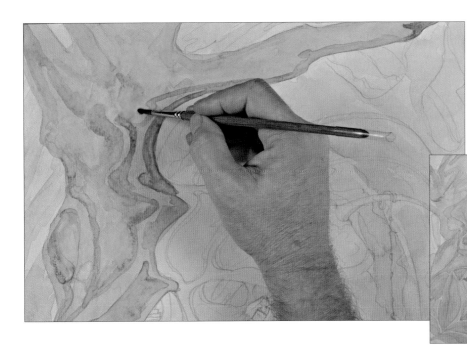

6 Using viridian hue only, darken some sections of the tree trunk further, following the curves on the drawing. Take the paint into the underside of the upper branch, and into the foreground branches on the right.

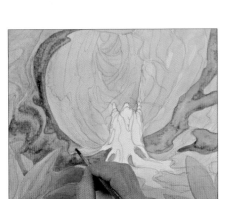

7 Strengthen the base of the trunk further using sap green and viridian hue. Apply the two colours separately, following closely the curved patterns on the drawing, and allow them to blend into each other naturally.

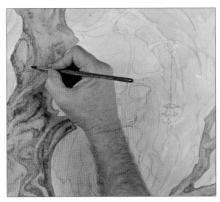

8 Continue these colours up to the top of the main trunk.

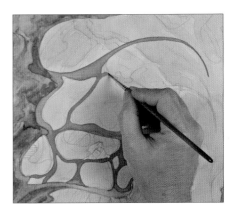

9 Change to the size 4 round brush and paint in the outer frame of the balcony using yellow ochre.

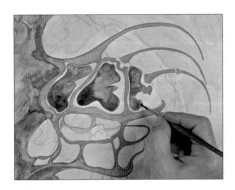

10 Use phthalo blue mixed with viridian hue for the three sections of the roof. Dab on a fairly wet mix, blending it so that it is darker at the bottom than at the top.

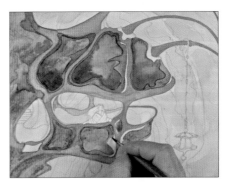

11 Continue laying the base colours on the balcony – viridian hue for the lower parts, and burnt sienna around each of the coloured sections.

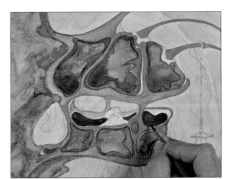

12 For the inside of the balcony, paint the lower part using alizarin crimson darkened towards the bottom with a touch of phthalo blue. Dry with a hairdryer.

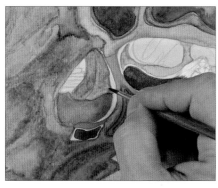

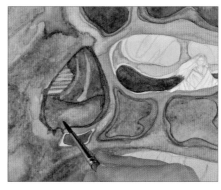

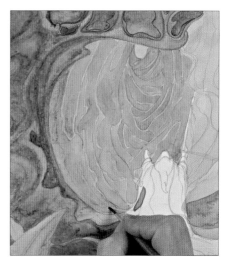

13 Paint the floor of the stairwell using yellow ochre darkened at the edges with Vandyke brown. Dry the paint with a hairdryer, then use viridian hue to paint the wall. Lay on a light mix followed by a darker mix to strengthen the colour.

14 Build up the shadows using indigo on the wall and burnt umber on the floor and around the entrance. Soften in the shadows using a clean, damp brush.

15 Use sap green and viridian hue to build up the colour on the inner walls of the cavern. Begin at the back of the cave and work forwards, section by section, leaving a narrow, unpainted border around each. Apply the two colours separately and blend them on the paper to achieve a varied background.

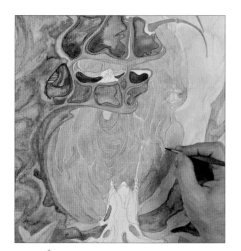

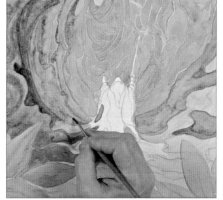

16 Continue into the outer part of the cavern on the left, and behind the balcony.

17 Strengthen the left-hand side of the cavern behind the tree, which is in shadow, using darker mixes of the two greens. Create the strong mottled effect by dabbing on patches of the two colours randomly and blending them together at the edges.

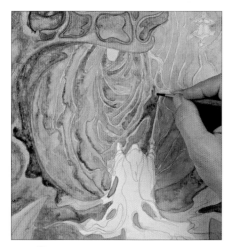

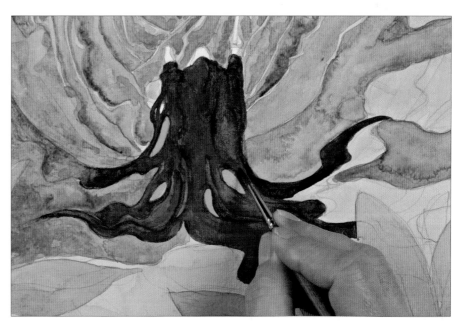

18 Continuing with the stronger mixes, darken the shaded parts of the inner cavern.

19 Mix together alizarin crimson and phthalo blue and paint the wizard's cloak. Build up the shadows in the folds of the cloak using phthalo blue, and blend the edges of the cloak into the background.

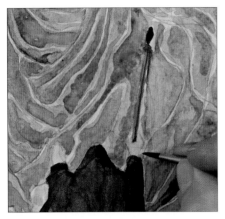

20 Use yellow ochre for the wizard's staff, and place a cobalt blue jewel on the end and a collar of alizarin crimson. Place a shadow down the right-hand side using burnt umber. Also use burnt umber for the wizard's hair, and a mix of white gouache and yellow ochre for his hands.

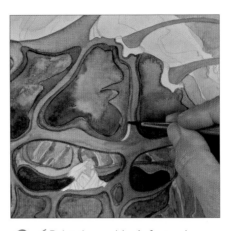

21 Paint the maiden's face using the same mix. Add the darker areas of the inner part of the balcony using a mix of burnt umber and burnt sienna. Use the same mix to complete the borders around the roof sections, and strengthen the outline.

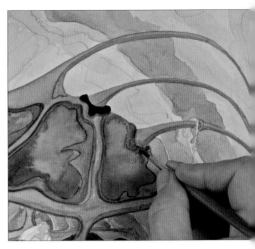

22 Apply the mix of burnt umber and burnt sienna to the undersides of the extensions to create shadow, and paint in the collars around their bases using alizarin crimson.

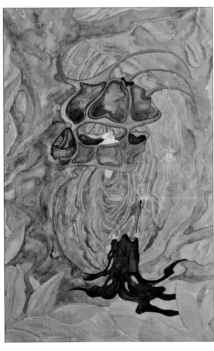

23 Strengthen the remainder of the background using sap green and viridian hue.

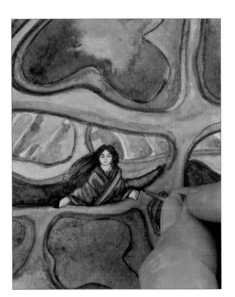

24 Change to a size 1 round brush and paint the figure on the balcony. Use phthalo blue for her cloak, lamp black for her hair and white gouache mixed with yellow ochre for the hands. Define the face and darken the folds in the cloak using burnt umber. With a size 0000 brush, use the same brown to paint on the face, strengthen the outline and add shadows to the hands. Add white highlights to the maiden's face, cloak and hair.

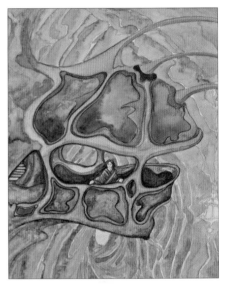

25 Using sepia and the size 1 round brush, continue to strengthen the outline of the balcony and the shadows within it.

TIP

Build up and strengthen the colours in your painting as many times as necessary to achieve the desired result. Accentuate the shadows and add white highlights to give your painting depth and bring it to life. Soften in the colours as you work using a clean, damp brush.

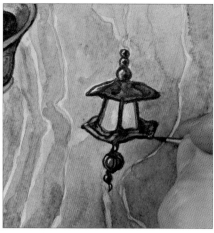

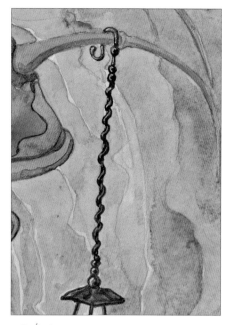

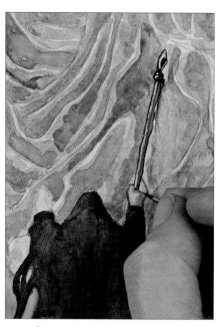

26 Paint the windows of the lantern using cadmium yellow. Add a white glow to each one. For the lantern itself, use burnt sienna and outline it in sepia; for the jewels use alizarin crimson and phthalo blue. Complete the lantern by adding cadmium yellow highlights to the lower rim and sharp white highlights here and there for added shine.

27 For the chain, put in the main cord first using burnt umber, then the chain wrapped around it using burnt sienna. Use Payne's gray for the hook, and add a sepia outline to the hook and the chain. Finish by adding white highlights.

28 Place a white highlight on the left-hand side of the wizard's staff, including the blue jewel, and strengthen the outline of the staff and the details on the wizard's hands using sepia.

29 Strengthen the outline of the wizard's cloak using Payne's gray, then change to the size 4 brush and add another layer of alizarin crimson. Darken the deepest folds using phthalo blue. Put some white highlights on the hands and hair.

30 Using Hooker's green, darken one side of each leaf, painting from the centre outwards to suggest veins.

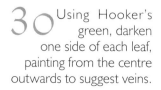

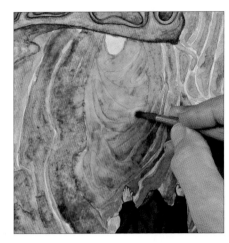

31 Add a hint of veining to the other side of each leaf. Mix together some Hooker's green, sap green and phthalo blue to make a dark green and use it to outline the leaves with the size 1 brush. Create a slightly serrated edge. Use the same colour to strengthen the veins where necessary. Brush in a little yellow ochre here and there in-between the veins to brighten the foliage.

32 Use the same dark green mix to darken the background behind the leaves, pushing them forwards. Blend it into the rest of the background.

33 Change to the size 6 brush and darken the inner part of the cavern using a mix of alizarin crimson and yellow ochre.

TIP

At this point I decided to place the main source of light at the far end of the inner cavern, drawing the eye into the centre of the painting, so I lightened the walls by lifting out colour. Placing light sources where, in reality, you would not expect them adds a sense of mystery and drama to a fantasy landscape.

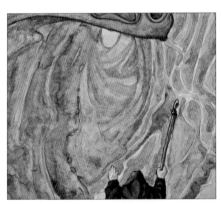

34 Dampen the far end of the cave with clean water and lift out the colour with a piece of kitchen paper to lighten it (see page 24).

35 Softly redefine the sections using a mix of Vandyke brown and Hooker's green and the size 1 brush. Dry with a hair dryer.

36 Use the same mix to strengthen the outline of the tree trunk using a size 3 brush. Deepen the shadows on the trunk with a paler version of the same mix, extending the shading behind the wizard's cloak and along the branch on the right of the picture to strengthen it.

37 Deepen the shadows on the cloak using alizarin crimson and blend it into the background.

38 Continue, using the same mix, to delineate the roots and branches within the cavern.

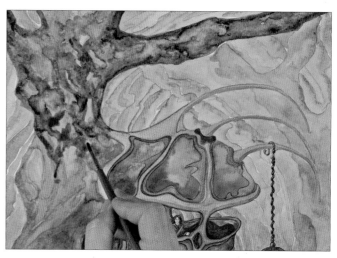

39 Change to the size 6 brush and, with a watery version of the same mix, build up the colour and texture of the main trunk, starting at the top. To create a strong, gnarled effect, dab the paint on in patches and drop in some clean water here and there. Place strong shadows either side of the trunk and the upper branch and soften them in.

40 Continue to create the same effect down the length of the trunk. Blend the green into the balcony to meld it to the tree.

41 Using white gouache mixed with a little sap green and the size 1 brush, add highlights to the inner cavern. Place them along the upper edge of each section and in the bright area at the far end. Soften the highlights in with a damp brush.

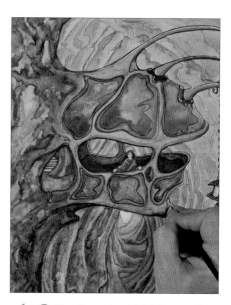

42 Continue the highlights on the sections of the cavern behind the balcony. Using burnt umber, deepen the darkest shadows on the roof of the balcony and sharpen the outline. Place strong white highlights along the top of the extensions and at various points on the edges of the balcony to brighten it.

TIP

Do not complete one feature or area of your painting at a time; move around from one to another, gradually strengthening shadows, building up colour and adding detail as you work, in order to gain a sense of how the picture, as a whole, is developing.

43 Place a white glow around the lantern and blend it into the background.

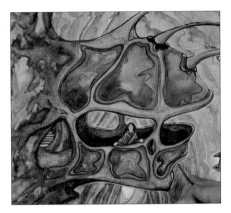

44 Place a sharp white highlight around the base of the balcony and the right-hand side to lift it away from the background.

45 Using cadmium red, add a ribbon at the corner of the balcony. Mix some phthalo blue with the red and put in a shadow along the lower edge. Place white highlights along the upper edge and blend them in.

TIP

The sparkle at the tip of the wizard's staff adds a magical finishing touch to this fantasy landscape.

47 Using a clean, damp size 3 brush, soften out the veining on the leaves a little and then intensify the background behind them with a light wash of sap green.

46 Place a sharp white highlight around the top part of the wizard's body, as if he is illuminated from the front, and down the left-hand side of the staff. At the top of the staff add a magical sparkle – first place a white dot in the centre with a small ring around it, then pull out the rays using a clean, slightly damp brush.

TIP

Adding a sharp white highlight around an object or deepening the background behind it are both devices that you can use to pull a feature out of the background and give it more prominence. The overall effect is to give more depth to a painting.

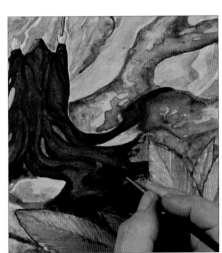

48 Darken the background on the right-hand side of the picture with a mix of viridian and sap green.

49 Complete the picture by deepening the shadows under the wizard's cloak using viridian and blending the edges of the cloak still further into the background.

Mystic Waterfall

I wanted to capture an ethereal, other-worldly atmosphere in this painting. The palette was kept muted and there is much less detail overall than in the previous two projects. The style is reminiscent of a Japanese painting. The size and scale of the waterfall is suggested by the building and the tiny figures beside it. By not showing the bottom of the waterfall, how much further down the mountain it falls is left completely to your imagination.

Painting water can seem rather daunting at first. Aim to achieve a sense of movement and luminosity. Still water will often reflect the colour of the sky, whereas moving water will produce spray and foam. In this painting I wanted to give the sense of water falling from a great height, but also that the viewer is a long way from the waterfall itself so that details are indistinct.

TIP

Remember to stretch your watercolour paper before starting the project (see page 8).

1 Draw the image directly on to the watercolour paper using a sharp F pencil, or transfer the image following the instructions on page 18. Use a set square and a ruler to ensure the ground level and the waterfall are straight.

YOU WILL NEED

300gsm (140lb) cold pressed
  NOT paper, size A3 (30 x
  42cm; 11¾ x 16½in)

F grade drawing pencil

Putty eraser

Paintbrushes: ⅝in (16mm) flat
  brush; sizes 1, 3, 4 and 6
  round brushes

Kitchen paper

Hairdryer

Water pot

Old toothbrush

Watercolour paints: ultramarine,
  phthalo blue, Payne's gray,
  indigo, yellow ochre,
  viridian hue, Vandyke brown,
  Chinese white

Gouache: permanent white

2 Make a fairly watery mix of ultramarine and, using a size 6 round brush, put in the deep blue sky. Start at the top of the painting and pull the colour down to the tops of the trees. Fade it out at the edges of the painting and above the waterfall using a clean, damp brush. When you are satisfied with the depth of colour obtained, dry the paint with a hairdryer.

TIP

Interesting effects can be obtained by dabbing on wet paint in patches and allowing it to spread randomly on the paper. Experiment with this technique to get a feel for how paint behaves and how to control it.

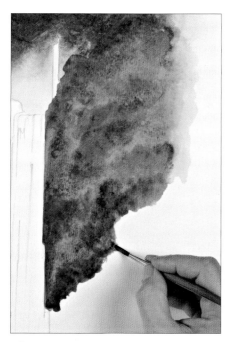

3 Using fairly thick mixes of phthalo blue and viridian hue, put in the tops of the trees on the cliff. Dab the colours on randomly in patches, blending them together on the paper to create a mottled effect. Work first on the right-hand side of the picture, fading the colours out towards the right.

4 Lift out any excess colour at the edges using a piece of kitchen paper (see page 24).

5 Paint the left-hand side of the picture in the same way and dry it with a hairdryer.

6 Lay a light wash of phthalo blue over the trees at the base of the waterfall on the left, fading it out gradually towards the bottom of the picture. Strengthen the tops of the trees with a mix of phthalo blue and a little indigo.

7 Using a stronger mix of the same colours, paint the trees on the right of the picture. Blend in some patches of viridian hue. The darker colours will pull the trees further forwards, into the foreground. Pull the colours down into the top of the cliff and fade it out at the edges of the picture using a damp brush.

8 Make a fairly watery mix of Payne's gray and phthalo blue, and use the size 4 brush to put in the rocks on the right. Paint carefully around the edge of the waterfall.

TIP

Fading out the paint at the sides of the picture gives it a mystical, dream-like quality; there are no sharp lines to detract from the soft focus of the piece. This is sometimes referred to as a vignette. It has the sense of being lifted out from another, larger painting to illustrate a specific part of a story.

9 Fade out the edges of the rocks using a clean, damp brush and strengthen the shadows to add depth and texture. Blend some white gouache into the lower parts of the rocks to soften them into the background.

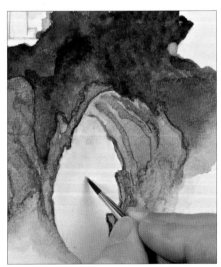

10 Lighten the roof of the cave a little using white gouache. Put a pale wash of phthalo blue and viridian hue over the space under the arch, then add a little white to the mix and put this in at the bottom.

11 Mix some white gouache with yellow ochre and place a light wash of colour over the temple.

12 blue behind the columns, and add some white highlights to the roof, base and columns.

13 Allow the paint to dry, then strengthen the colour and the highlights where necessary. Add stronger shadows inside the temple using Vandyke brown mixed with a little yellow ochre.

14 Put in a pale wash of Payne's gray mixed with phthalo blue beneath the waterfall, then use the same mix to add streaks of colour to the waterfall itself. Also add some pale streaks of phthalo blue; both colours will be softened in later.

15 Lay a thin wash of white gouache over the waterfall to soften in the blue and the grey. Apply the paint in long, vertical brush strokes. Blend the paint into the area at the base of the waterfall.

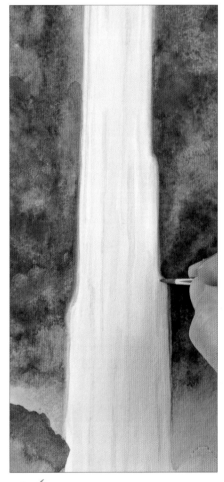

16 Continue to strengthen the white, softening it in using a clean, damp brush. Ensure you maintain a well-defined, straight edge to the waterfall as you work, blending it in slightly with the greens either side.

18 Lay a weak wash of phthalo blue over the waterfall using the edge of the flat brush and, once applied, use a dry brush to blend it in. Work in the same direction as the flow of the water. Vary the tone slightly as you work, and introduce touches of indigo and Payne's gray here and there.

TIP

When painting water, try and let the luminescence of the paper show through the paint. Use long, flowing strokes and highlight spray splashes with white gouache. Water naturally takes on the colour of its surroundings, the sky, or the kind of rock that it is flowing over, but of course in a fantasy painting your 'water' can be any colour you wish!

17 Lay some white gouache around the roof of the temple and blend it into the background. Use the tip of the brush to pull out some rays of light. If the white is too harsh, dampen it with a light wash of water to recede it into the background, leaving just a suggestion of light.

19 Mix some yellow ochre with a little white gouache and use a size 3 round brush to put in the tower at the top of the cliff. Blend it in, then add a white highlight down the left-hand side and a Vandyke brown shadow on the right.

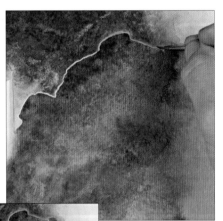

20 Create a glow around the tops of the trees on the right by painting in a thin band of white using the tip of the brush. Blend it into the background.

TIP

By lightening the horizon I have tried to suggest a bright light source beyond the trees. It could be the rising moon, or something else entirely! This helps add to the ethereal atmosphere and delineates the trees from the sky itself. Their tonal values are fairly close and this helps just bring the trees forward slightly.

21 Repeat on the left-hand side.

22 Place a similar white glow around the left-hand side of the trees at the bottom of the picture on the right, and then use Payne's gray mixed with a little indigo to paint in the two tiny figures standing on the top of the cliff.

TIP

To add spray and mist, use the technique known as 'spattering'. Cover the parts of the picture you do not want to spatter with roughly torn pieces of tissue paper. Load an old toothbrush with generous amounts of white gouache. Angle the toothbrush downwards and, holding it approximately 5cm (2in) from the surface of the paper, rub your thumb over the bristles, flicking paint on to your painting. Any over-large drops can be lifted out using kitchen paper.

23 Build up the waterfall further using more white gouache, softening it in as you work.

24 Strengthen the colour on the temple using yellow ochre mixed with a little white gouache, and sharpen the edge of the dome. Accentuate the white highlights using the tip of the brush, and deepen the shadows with Vandyke brown.

25 Work more white paint into the waterfall. Use smaller, more closely defined brush strokes to achieve a sense of flowing water. Soften and blend in the colour as you work.

26 Use Chinese white to lay a light, translucent wash over the temple, giving it a magical glow.

27 Place a sparkle at the top of the tower. Use a size 1 brush and white gouache, and begin with a central dot surrounded by a ring of white. Pull out the rays from the middle using a clean, damp brush to complete the picture.

Temple on the Lake

The symmetry of this peaceful scene is broken only by the alien moons. The depth and stillness of the water are suggested by the reflection, which is virtually a mirror-image of the real thing – only the horizontal lines painted in white gouache across the water and the use of paler mixes for the reflection tell us which is which.

Index